Forever 19

Heidi Sallee

Published by Heidi Sallee, 2024.

While every precaution has been taken in the preparation of this book, the publisher assumes no responsibility for errors or omissions, or for damages resulting from the use of the information contained herein.

FOREVER 19

First edition. October 1, 2024.

Copyright © 2024 Heidi Sallee.

ISBN: 979-8224420261

Written by Heidi Sallee.

Acknowledgements

I am forever grateful for those who voluntarily relived the horror of Emali's death, and those who generously shared their own experiences, thereby making this book possible.

My thoughts, sympathies, and wishes for healing will remain with those whose grief was too overwhelming for them to participate.

Rebecca, for the love, and the help, and for abiding throughout.

Joshua, for assuming the role of my backbone, knowing my limits for me, and picking up the slack.

Logan, for always being there and allowing me to grieve with the perfect amount of support.

Sarah and Nadia, for taking care of my home when I could not.

Sophia, who created the shirts and the key chains in Emali's honor.

Everyone who has supported me while I created this book. Please don't think that your efforts went unnoticed, or were taken for granted - or that I will ever forget.

Dedication

For Elianna

Foreword

On April 10th, 2024, nineteen-year-old Emali Renee Sallee was killed by her boyfriend.

This book contains the memories, thoughts, and opinions of those who were closest to her, as well as commentary from others who understand her situation. You might take notice of the absence of some people whom you might expect to see here; however, we ask that you avoid forming any opinions about them because of their silence. Everyone has their individual reactions to tragedy, and we all deal with loss in our own ways. For some, the pain runs too deep for them to verbalize it, let alone share it with others, and we ask the reader to respect their wishes and keep them in your thoughts.

You'll likely sense a wide range of feelings and emotions, such as guilt, sorrow, regret, and outrage. Of these, we will tap as strongly as possible into the outrage - because that anger is what will change the current climate of violence and its countless ways of destroying lives.

This book is written with the hope of being a fitting tribute to Emali, but it also carries with it a fervent desire and a perpetual prayer that by the time Emali's little girl reads this, she will live in a world where this kind of tragedy is our history, and not our reality. We want to be able to look Emali's daughter in the eyes and say, "This is what life was like back then, but your mother's life changed all that."

Although we will forever mourn the loss of Emali, we want to be able to look back on this time and say that her death was senseless, but not without meaning - that it was as cruel as it was heartbreaking, but incepted a greater hope and a better future for women everywhere.

It was final, but certainly not the end.

This is also intended to be a cautionary tale, a warning that no one is completely safe; further, it is a plea to women everywhere that when loved ones are expressing their concerns about your relationship, you need to listen to them.

Thanks to the efforts of those who have worked unceasingly to bring Domestic Violence into the light, everyone is aware of the abuse in our culture, and the fact that it has become far too common. It's well past time to move beyond the statistics and on to the solutions, some of which we'll explore here. More than anything else, though, people need to understand - and then believe - that yes, it *can* happen to you or to someone you care about. And you need to get involved, because awareness is absolutely meaningless without action.

In other words, the reality of Domestic Violence is a testimony to the old saying, "If you aren't part of the solution, you're part of the problem."

This book is offered to remember Emali, to support the loved ones she was forced to leave behind, and to find the answers we so desperately need.

Heidi Sallee

August, 2024

Heidi
Emali's mom

"It isn't 'drama'. It's safety."

ONE OF THE MEMORIES that I try to keep at bay - even though I fail to do so - is the entirety of the day before Emali was murdered.

My daughter was still here, still with us, still living her life. Actually, she had gone to Bangor the weekend before to see friends, and perhaps clear her head enough to make a decision about her boyfriend, whom she wanted to escape. I was tentatively hopeful that she would use the time away to realize the truth of her situation.

When she came back on the night of Sunday, April 7th, I asked her how she was doing. It turned out that while she was in Bangor, her boyfriend had been calling her, texting her, seemingly attempting to continue what I regarded as his pattern of controlling Emali. Isolating her. She had previously told me about his habit of guilting her into cancelling plans with friends and family, haranguing her about any amount of time that she wanted to be away from him until eventually, she would give in to his demands. When she finally took a few days away from him, she arrived at the place in her mind where she simply wasn't going to take it anymore. She told me that she was done.

That was what I'd been waiting for, hoping for - because she knew quite well that I didn't like her relationship with him; however, my initial protests about him seemed to cause Emali to pull back from me, so I took a different approach. I tried to keep the lines of communication open with her through more indirect methods: I was consistently there for her to talk to, and I made sure she knew I *always* would be there for whatever she needed. I was careful to acknowledge her perspectives and her opinions, I was less intrusive, but I kept the conversation going through sharing relevant stories and social media with her. And I lived with that constant, hypervigilant, static-like buzzing in the back of my mind that came from knowing that Emali wasn't safe.

So when she told me she was leaving him, a huge weight lifted from my shoulders - but some of the heaviness remained, because the next step was for Emali to get her things from the place they shared, and the idea of it scared me.

Emali's plan was to use her next day off to pack her things and move back home to us. She would leave him for good on Wednesday, April 10th. She didn't want any help, didn't want anyone to stand by for protection, didn't want any drama. I was nervous on the ninth, even more so on the tenth, thinking about how it wasn't about avoiding drama. It was about being safe.

The last time I spoke to my daughter was at 4:14 p.m. on April 10th, 2024. At some point after that, the boyfriend shot Emali, killing her. He then killed himself.

In deciding to murder Emali and then commit suicide, he left her two-year-old daughter with no parents at all.

As things stand, my granddaughter lives with me, and I'll forever mourn the fact that she won't get to grow up with the mother who loved her endlessly. I doubt that my granddaughter will even remember her mother, since she's so young. One of the purposes of this book is to keep Emali's memory alive for her daughter. I want her to have something of her mother.

I can say that I miss my daughter, but that simple statement does absolutely no justice to the silenced, still place in my heart, the place where my love for Emali lives on. It's a constant ache. The worst of it is in the morning, when I'm almost fully awake and I remember that she's not here, and I feel that sudden jolt of grieving.

But I get up and I start my day. Life is somehow going on without Emali, but it's like someone came into my life and amputated my arm. My reaction to that would be worse than missing it, longing for it: Beyond the anger, there would be times when I'd swear I could still feel it there, even though my rational mind would know that it was gone.

I suppose we learn to live with tragedy and injustice and pain, but life is altered, and it will never be the same.

I said in an interview that not many voices are being raised against Domestic Violence. I've rethought that a bit. There are people talking about it; however, not nearly enough people even understand it, let alone take action to address it. I know that there are many tentacles of DV that I don't understand, either; moreover, if I'm completely honest, I wonder at times if perhaps I don't *want* to know. Maybe I'm equating a full comprehension of this lunacy with some kind of personal assimilation - like if I truly understand the mind of the batterer, especially one turned murderer, I'll be contaminated by the evil.

But seeing as Emali has now paid the ultimate, eternal price for the senseless and selfish entitlement of an angry male - and by proxy, everyone who loved her will forever pay for his crimes, as well - I want to understand what's going on here. I want to know not only what happened to my little girl, but *why* it happened.

Then, I want to do something about it. For real. Something that will actually work, because in spite of all the people talking, it doesn't seem to be getting any better.

Becca

Emali's friend, and close friend of the family

YOU KNOW, YOU HEAR about these tragedies way, *way* too often. It's always shocking. Before Emali's murder, I know that whenever I would see yet another story about a woman being murdered by her partner, it hit me like a sudden slap in the face, and I would think about it for a while. I would shake my head and wonder what the hell was *wrong* with these guys. Eventually, the horror of it would blend into the background of my thoughts, and life would go on.

Then April 10th, 2024 happened, and Emali was dead. She was gunned down by the father of her baby as she was trying to pack her things and move out of the house they shared.

Once the initial shock abated a bit, the truth of this evil that we call "domestic violence" came into devastatingly sharp focus for me. And the shift in my perspective - not only regarding abuse, but many facets of life overall - was tectonic. You know about those pivotal events in life, the ones where people can tell you exactly where they were and what they were doing at the moment they found out what happened?

April 11th, the day after, will always be one of mine. I'm sure that's true for anyone who knew Emali.

On that day, Emali's mom and I were at the bowling center where we work, all excited for the fact that the staff was getting new T-shirts. On our way to pick them up, Emali called, and Heidi stepped outside to talk to her. It turned out that Emali needed her mom to pick up the baby from day care because Emali was ending the relationship with her daughter's father, moving out, and she was a bit overwhelmed from dealing with him and with trying to get her things and get out. She told her mom that it would take longer than she'd thought.

Confused - because she didn't really understand what was going on at that moment - Heidi took me back to work and then hurriedly left to get the baby. I found out later that Heidi began to worry that evening when Emali didn't text to check on her daughter. Emali was an amazing mother, known for keeping close tabs on anything and everything concerning her child; yet on that night, there was no communication at all. Her habit was to text or call consistently whenever she was away from her child, checking on how she was doing, how much she'd eaten, asking for pictures. But Emali had gone silent.

I later learned that Emali's best friend, Kyra, had gone to Emali's place to check on her. Kyra knocked on the door, but there was no response. She called Heidi, concerned that the lights were on in the house and the cars were in the driveway, but the curtains were drawn and no one was coming to the door. That was when Kyra called the police for a welfare check.

The next day, April 11th, I was helping out at a local restaurant. I had gone in to manage the staff, since they were low on managers and I used to work there. At 10:18 a.m., my phone dinged with a text from the owner of the bowling center where Heidi and I worked.

It said, *When you have a minute, I need to talk to you.*

I texted back that no, I actually didn't have a minute, because I was managing the staff through the breakfast rush. I asked him if it was important.

He replied with, *I need you to call me.*

At this point, I was pissed off. We were slamming busy, one of the servers was running late, the kitchen was backed up, and there were only three of us at that moment running the front of the house.

So when I called him, I wasn't at all polite. I felt that what I was doing at that moment was far more important than a random call from my other boss, and I was overtly rude to him. Why that sticks in my mind, I really don't know - but I've apologized more than once for my attitude on that day, and it still bothers me.

When he picked up, I snapped, "What *is* it?"

"Please sit down, Becca," he answered calmly, but there was a definite edge to his tone.

"No, I can't sit down. I have a restaurant full of people, I'm in charge of seven staff, I have no time for this, so what do you need?"

"Becca, sit down."

There was something in his voice, an odd tone to it that I'd never heard before. I was plenty irritated, but I moved to the area where we kept the high chairs and perched myself on the edge of one of them.

"Okay. I'm sitting."

He hesitated for only a moment, then said, "Emali's been shot."

My childhood best friend is named "Emily." She was the one I thought of.

"What? *What?*"

"Heidi's daughter has been shot."

You would think that such a statement might take a minute to sink in, but my legs went to rubber immediately, and I sank to the floor.

"What are you talking about?" It was hard to get the words out. I felt like all the oxygen was suddenly sucked out of the room.

He repeated it, and I dove into denial.

I said, "That's not funny. Why would you say that? That is *so* not funny..."

I remember the sharpness in his voice then. He needed me to hear him.

"I'm *not joking*, Becca. You need to get to Heidi's house. You're family to them, and you need to go. *Now*."

I started crying. I hung up and escaped into the back office while feeling myself go absolutely numb - like all the way to my core, just this icy numbness that made me unsteady on my feet.

In the office, I called Heidi to find out which hospital I should go to.

"I'm leaving work now," I said. "Which hospital is she at?"

"What do you mean?"

"The hospital. I'm heading to the hospital - where are we going?"

"Becca..."

"What's going on? Where are we meeting? Where is she?"

"We aren't going to the hospital, Becca. I need you to come here. To the house."

"There's no *time* - what are you talking about?"

Then came the three words that will haunt me for the rest of my life:

"She's dead, Becca."

My knees buckled again, and I quickly sat down as I hung up and my coworker rushed in, concerned.

She asked me what was going on, and I told her I had to go. It truly didn't matter to me anymore what was going on around me; actually, I believed then - as I do now - that the entire world needed to stop for a while. Just *stop*. It felt like I was being sucked into a vortex, and if the world would hold still for a minute, maybe I'd be able to crawl out.

She followed me as I hurried to the front of the restaurant.

"You can't go," she said. "You're managing. We don't have enough people here..."

"I have to go."

She was holding on to my shoulders, trying to make eye contact.

"You can't drive like this - what's going on?"

"Emali. Emali's dead."

The words didn't sound real, even to me.

"What? What are you saying?"

I tried to take a deep breath, but that wasn't happening. I pulled away from her and quietly said, "I need you to keep a straight face. Don't show anything."

I looked around at the customers, so many of them the regulars who loved Emali, loved Heidi, and had become part of the fabric of their lives. I had a fleeting thought about what they would think and feel when they found out, and I couldn't bear it.

"Until I know exactly what's going on, just hold things down here."

"Okay." She nodded. "Okay."

It just now occurred to me how strong she was on that awful day. I need to tell her that.

I ran out to my car. I don't remember the trip to Heidi's house very well; actually, I've blocked out several parts of that day. But I do remember pulling up to the house and seeing the sheriff's car there, parked in front like a silent sentry, announcing to the neighborhood that something awful had happened.

Up to that point, I was still hoping that there was some kind of mistake. I had even toyed with the idea that it was all a cruel, unfathomable joke or something. I was praying to God that someone, somewhere had made a terrible blunder, and it would all be sorted out and everything would be fine. We would all be fine. A life simply cannot end so suddenly, with no warning, with no time to affect the outcome.

It was starting to sink in, though. Two horrible phone conversations. The police car at Heidi's house. The base knowledge I had that these people wouldn't lie to me. The more it registered with me, the more surreal everything around me became.

The sheriff pulled me aside as I approached the house, asking who I was and why I was there, then telling me he needed to talk to me.

I shook my head. "I need to see Heidi."

"No, in a minute. She knows what's going on. You need to know, as well."

He explained what had happened the night before, how they had gone for another welfare check early that morning and found them dead, went to get Heidi from her job, and how crushed she was when they told her. He wanted me to be as prepared as possible for what I would find when I saw Heidi, and I'm glad he took the time to do that.

As I went into the house, I thought of the happy times I'd spent there. I was always at the house, often enough that I never knocked, just walked in. They would joke about my responsibility to discipline Emali's little brother. When he acted up or got in trouble for something, Heidi would say to me, "You need to go do something about your son, Becca." I love that kid. So much.

And now someone had killed his big sister. I was starting to get a nauseating sense of how far the tentacles of this tragedy would reach.

I could hear Heidi before I saw her. She was kind of screaming, but not a full shriek - not like that. The sound she was making was like a breathy, quiet scream, if there is such a thing.

Our eyes locked, and the first thing she said was, "She wanted to be a willow tree."

I didn't know what to say to that. I had no idea what she was talking about.

"A *willow* tree, Becca. She wanted to be a willow tree." Before I could respond, she added, "The baby. We need to get the baby from daycare."

"We'll do that, Heidi. We'll go get the baby." Heidi's ex - Emali's father, Dave - was in the house, as were Emali's sister and little brother, so I knew we'd need to get that done quickly.

The officer was talking to us about the next steps, advising that they would at some point release the house Emali had been sharing with the baby's father, and telling us what we needed to do in order to get emergency guardianship of Emali's daughter. I think it was then that he told us the initial investigation was revealing a probable murder-suicide, and again, that surreal feeling washed over me. It simply wasn't registering. I hadn't even thought about Emali's boyfriend to that point - only Emali, and here was the revelation that they were both dead.

I was part of Emali's family. I'd known her for years, yet I had never met her boyfriend. He never seemed interested in getting to know any of us.

The sheriff said they would release the house to us first, so we could clear out Emali's belongings and get what her daughter needed. I looked at Heidi and said, "I love you, but I can't go there. To that house. I can't do that."

She just nodded and answered, "Okay. That's okay, Becca."

I look back at that moment now and wonder how I could have been so selfish, and how Heidi could have been so gracious.

A short while after, Dave and I left. He was going to get Heidi's car from where she worked, so I gave him a ride over there. Then I was going to go back to the restaurant to explain to my boss what was happening. For some reason that I'll probably never understand, I was moving too fast, driving too fast - even my thoughts were racing through my head with no real structure or purpose. I mean, what was the hurry? The world had collapsed. I could change nothing. It was done. I think maybe I was trying to somehow outrun reality.

I went in to the bowling center after I dropped Dave off. I just wanted to talk to my boss, the man who had called me at the restaurant and told me about Emali. I was furious, but not at him: I was trying to figure out what we'd missed. There were indicators that we didn't pick up on. There *had* to be, and I needed to figure out what they were. I needed some time to think.

And I wasn't ready to face anyone at the restaurant. I didn't want to talk about it with them, not yet. Both Heidi and Emali used to work there, and it was going to hit everyone like a brick wall falling on their heads. I knew they would have questions. I had no answers.

More than anything else, though, I went inside the center because I needed a hug.

The first person I saw when I walked in was the other manager, who greeted me with this expression on his face that was a mixture of disbelief and compassion, and then the simple statement, "I heard."

I curled up on the floor in a seated fetal position and sobbed. I felt like I would never be able to stop.

He was worried about me trying to drive, wanted to call my boyfriend, but I refused. I just needed a little time to get my legs under me. Heidi needed me back at the house, and I wanted to be as together as possible before I went back there.

After I calmed down, I stopped at the restaurant on my way to Heidi's house, asking the staff to meet me in the kitchen. I kept it as brief and as simple as I could.

"Emali's been killed," I said. I could actually feel the jolt that went through the room, so I hurried to continue:

"They're still investigating, so I don't have a lot of information for you all. We're going to go get the baby and then I'll be at Heidi's house, so you guys finish up here. I'm going to ask the higher-ups if we can close for the night."

Through their gasps and their tears, I heard a couple of them say they needed to call Heidi, but I warned them against blowing up her phone at that moment. "If you really want to talk to her, go to the house. She needs that kind of in-person support, not phone calls. And keep your questions to a minimum, because we don't fully know what happened yet."

Our GM had arrived. I explained the situation to him, and he asked, "Becca, why are you here?"

"I thought..."

"No." He shook his head. "Go. Nothing here even matters. Go do whatever you need to do."

I looked around at the shattered faces of my coworkers, the shock and concern in my manager's eyes, and that was finally my moment of full realization. I had been clinging to a scrap of hope that it was a mistake. I'd been experiencing that impulse that we all have in the face of unimaginable tragedy - the mostly-buried and completely futile thought that it can be fixed, it isn't forever, our loved one will be back.

And I thought, *It's real. It happened. This actually is our new reality.*

AS I ENTERED HEIDI'S home, I saw a man there whom I didn't recognize. He came over to me and hugged me, thanking me for being there.

I pulled away and snapped, "I don't know who you are."

"That's my brother, Becca," Heidi said softly. "Remember? It's Josh."

Her phone rang with a call from the State Police, informing us that they had released the house, so we could enter it at that point to get Emali's and the baby's things.

They suggested that it might not be a good idea for Heidi to go into that house - for obvious reasons - and the same would be true for Emali's little sister and brother. I felt my gut grip as Heidi and I looked at each other and I understood what needed to be done.

Josh and I left for Minot, where the house was. Josh rode with me. I've seen grown men cry before, but not like Josh was crying: He sobbed with his entire body. There was grief there, and the deepest sorrow; however, what I remember most was the rage I felt emanating from him, like it had burrowed into his very soul and was choking him.

When he'd calmed himself some, I asked him if he had known Emali's boyfriend.

He nodded. "I was about to go check on what was going on in that house when I got the call. I knew something bad was happening - Emali never would have dropped off the radar like that."

There was a state trooper in the driveway when we pulled up. He told us how sorry he was for our loss, then Josh explained why we were there.

"Of course." The officer pointed toward the back of the house. "You'll go in back there. The room where it happened is on the left, and that door is shut. Just go to the right. Everything should be in there."

Josh went in first. I was having trouble getting my feet to move to the back of the house, to the place where Emali and her daughter had lived. The place where Emali had been killed. I would have given an awful lot for a good reason to run, but there was none.

As it turned out, the door to the room where the murder had happened was left open, I think by Josh when he went in the first time.

I immediately noticed the stench. I can't really describe it, but if evil had a definitive smell, that would be it.

We got Emali's personal effects - her wallet, purse, etc. - and started gathering the things the baby would need. At some point, we called Heidi for reinforcements, because there was just too much in the house for us to get everything ourselves. The coworker who had been at the restaurant with me that morning arrived in record time.

Then I called my boss at the bowling center. He picked up on the first ring and asked, "What do you need?"

"You and your truck."

"We're on our way."

Those moments were the only comfort of that day. Good friends. Good, caring people who came running in our time of need. Unless something had blood on it, if it belonged to Emali or the baby, I wanted it to go with me. These wonderful people made sure that happened.

We did our best to finish before the boyfriend's mother showed up. We tried to keep in mind that she had also just lost her child, and she would want to collect her son's things, but we didn't want to see her. It was all too raw.

She did arrive after we'd been there for a couple of hours. She was quite upset, of course, and what was left of my rational mind understood that; still, I almost bit into my tongue a few times as we hurried to finish up.

On the way back to Heidi's, the thought occurred to me that I had gotten two more years of life than Emali did, and it slammed into my psyche like a blow to the head. To this day, I still grapple with my feelings about that - like if I can make sense out of it, I can stop feeling the guilt and the regret which I suspect will haunt me forever.

SEVERAL WEEKS HAVE gone by since that hideous day; and at this point, I'm mad at the world. That's the best way to describe it. I'm furious at and disgusted by the guy who killed Emali. I'm angry at anyone who knew him and what he was about and did nothing to help. Nothing to stop him.

I'm angry at myself for the clues I missed.

Emali was quiet about what was happening to her; but now, looking back, I think about April fifth. Emali had stopped by the bowling center where her mother and I work so she could drop off the baby, then head to Bangor for that weekend with her friends. While she was there with us, her phone was blowing up with calls from the boyfriend. She didn't have her phone on speaker, yet I could still hear him screaming at her. It was jarring, to say the least, and I remember being glad that she was going away for a few days. I wonder now what

I should have, *could* have said or done, but it never occurred to me that she would be dead at his hands a few days later.

I feel guilt over that. And I feel guilt for the times I spent with Emali's mom. It's like somehow I took time from them, time that I didn't know was dwindling, and was therefore precious.

I didn't fully realize how much Emali had withdrawn from her social contacts, or how isolated she was becoming. I wish I'd been paying more attention.

I'm outraged that Emali's little girl will grow up without her mom, but that's part of a bigger anger at the culture which, in my opinion, helped create her mother's death. Generally speaking, with as often as these murders happen, I have to wonder if we're raising girls to become women who are not only more accepting of abuse, but who maybe even accept it as something inevitable; further, I think a lot about how these males are growing up, as well. How they're being raised. Where are their parents? Are they making excuses for them, covering up for them, not holding them accountable for their misdeeds?

Do these parents realize what they're setting loose on the world?

So yes, I'm angry. The difference now is that I'm wake-up angry. My perspective has changed, and I've been learning a lot.

One of the things I've noticed lately, when talking about domestic violence, is how often blame is assigned to the victim. I especially hate that question, "Why don't abused women just *leave*?"

Maybe it's because she and her family are being threatened. Maybe a battered woman is protecting her children from being alone with an abuser, which is something she can do only by staying with him. Maybe when he isolates her sufficiently, she believes she has nowhere else to turn. Probably a mix of all those reasons, plus more; but let's be honest, these abusers aren't punished adequately. If, indeed, they are held accountable by the system, the worst they'll get is three hots and a cot for a while and maybe some anger management. I'd like to see them imprisoned for decades, especially when there are children involved -

because in spite of the current conventional "wisdom", I believe that any guy who has even the capability to batter the mother of his kids should have his parental rights terminated.

So that's how angry I am, and I hope I stay this way. My outrage will serve to help women, and to find solutions, plus one more thing - the most important thing:

It will help me keep Emali's daughter safe.

Eva
Emali's little sister

"I miss the family we once were."

SOMEONE RECENTLY ASKED me about my favorite memories of Emali.

At first, I drew a blank. I mean, she was my *sister*. We not only shared our lives, but we actually came into existence from the same life source. There was a bond there, woven into our souls - a closeness that can't be adequately described just through my memories of her.

Still, those memories are what I now rely on to keep her alive in my heart.

What I miss the most are the everyday moments that come from having my best friend just ten feet from my bedroom door. I miss the times when I would hang out with her in her room, or she would stroll into mine, and we would talk or watch a movie. We would have sleepovers - I loved those, because we would make silly TikToks and laugh like crazy. Or sometimes she would do my makeup. She was really good at that.

She became more withdrawn as we got older, though, especially in the months leading up to her death.

To be honest, I knew before anyone told me that Emali was gone. She had called me while I was at school, but I couldn't take the call at that time, so I called her back afterwards - around two o'clock p.m. on April 10th. She didn't answer for a while, but when I finally reached her, she said she was just calling to get someone to pick her daughter up from day care. She was going to pack up her things and leave her boyfriend that day. Then she told me she had gotten ahold of Mommy, so the baby was all set.

I didn't ask her anything about her boyfriend, about why she was leaving. Like I said, she'd become distant in recent months, and I didn't want to intrude.

Emali called me again around 4:15. I was at my Lacrosse practice and couldn't answer; however, I called her as soon as I got out, around 5:00. I was driving a friend to work in Sabattus - about a half-hour away from my high school - and I was calling her repeatedly on the trip. I had invited her to come with me to New York for the weekend, but she still hadn't told me if she could make it. I needed to know so I could book the hotel.

Besides, I was worried. Something felt off.

I kept calling her as I drove back home. She never answered.

My boyfriend came over that night, and by the time he got to my house, I was feeling anxious in a way I never did before. I was being rude, angry towards him, snapping at nothing at all. My head felt like a rubber band that was stretched too far. I tried to tell myself that I was just overtired, the day had been too busy and I just needed to get some sleep; but in the back of my mind, I knew that wasn't the problem at all.

I went straight to bed after my boyfriend left. I fell asleep relatively quickly, but woke up at three a.m. feeling nauseated. It's hard to describe. I was just very ill and very afraid. I managed to drift off again, then woke up at five o'clock, knowing I was up for the day at that point. And for reasons I wasn't fully aware of yet, I woke up crying.

I checked my phone. Emali still hadn't contacted me, but my mom had texted:

Have you heard from Emali?

I think I stopped breathing for a few moments, then I responded:

She's not here?

I saw there was another text from Mommy:

Kyra is going to the house to check on her.

I started to get ready for school that day, feeling robotic, just going through the motions. My mom came into my room around six-thirty. She was crying.

She sat on the floor while I perched at the end of my bed. I didn't know what to say or what to ask her, so I waited for her to speak.

She said, "Your sister isn't answering me."

The way she was wringing her hands is one of my most vivid memories of that day.

"I don't know what's going on," she was saying. "She didn't come home last night. She never checked on the baby. She *always* checks on the baby. The cops did a welfare check, they're doing another one now... Kyra said the lights were on but the door was locked and no one answered..."

The thought finally, fully announced itself to my brain, and I let it in. In that moment, I knew that Emali was dead. I've never experienced anything like that - a sudden knowledge of something, as real and as irrefutable as if the police had walked in and told us themselves.

The night before, when I was angry and my emotions were all over the place, I'd had this odd sensation of something lifting away from me. Emali and I were sisters. We were soul-tied. I understood then, with perfect clarity, what that feeling of release was: It was the moment of the untying. It was Emali's soul being freed from this life.

I couldn't tell Mommy that, of course. I couldn't even allow the thought to linger. I started telling myself that I was wrong; that yes, she was probably hurt or something, and she needed to go to the hospital. That was why she wasn't contacting anyone. But she would be okay.

So the only response I could come up with was, "We need to call Daddy."

My mom called him then. Daddy was upset, asking lots of questions about everything that had happened the night before, while I sat on my bed listening and praying.

A few minutes later, I told Mommy that I was going to get ready for school. I really didn't know how else to handle what was happening. I think I was kind of desperate to do something normal.

Yet I knew what the truth was. No amount of talking myself out of it was going to change what I already knew in my heart. And I needed to tell someone, needed to let it be out there, because we were all about to enter a hellish reality and I wanted to be as aware as possible, if that makes sense. I also needed someone to be there for me.

I got on my phone, on the group chat I had with my two closest friends, and told them I was just going to lay it out for them: My sister was dead.

Of course, they responded initially with confusion and disbelief, then shock. I got into my car and headed for the school, but something about telling them made everything very real, very fast, and I started screaming. Sobbing. I tried praying again, asking God to please let Emali be alive - even if she was injured, even hurt badly, we would help her. *Anything*, as long as she was alive.

At the school, I waited a solid half-hour before I could calm myself enough to go inside. During that time, one of my friends came out and got in beside me, asking what was happening.

"Emali hasn't responded to me since yesterday afternoon," I explained. "She's not answering anyone. Mommy called the cops, Kyra even went by the house but no one answered the door... All this stuff is happening, and she's not *answering* us. And the baby is staying at our house. That alone would make her call back asap, but she never even texted to check on her."

My friend and I prayed together, then the bell rang and we had to go inside. The only thing I brought with me was my Bible. I had only one class that day - Art class - and I spent it reading the Book of Matthew. I couldn't really focus, though. My thoughts were just so jumbled.

I got a call from one of my group-text friends, so I went out into the hallway to call her back. She is, by nature, a very chill, laid-back person. Very calm.

She insisted that Emali was fine, that there had to be an explanation for her falling out of touch and we'd find out what that reason was at some point.

As much as I wanted to agree with her, I couldn't. I went into greater detail about what had been going on since the day before. It occurred to me at that time that Emali would have needed to be awake and getting ready for work two hours earlier, yet she was still not answering any calls or texts, and I told my friend that. I needed her to be up to speed on the situation, because I was getting this panicky feeling - like I was standing there screaming in the middle of a room full of people, but no one could hear me. What I wanted from her, from anyone, I had no idea. I still don't. I was just trying to find a way to get my own mind around it, I guess.

I would find out later that at this point, the police had already forced entry to Emali's place and found their bodies.

I LEFT SCHOOL AND WENT to my job, which was at the same daycare center that Emali's daughter went to. I stayed close to my niece that day, trying to play with all of the children and do my other tasks, but there was all this noise in my head from the kids' music, the chatter of coworkers, and the children themselves. None of that would have bothered me on any other day; actually, I wouldn't even have noticed it much.

But pretty quickly into my shift, I started getting this sensation like I was floating. I don't know how else to describe it. I felt like my feet weren't really attached to the ground. Then my chest started to hurt, so badly that I couldn't catch my breath.

I'd never had an anxiety attack before. That one was the first, and I've been getting them ever since that day.

My Uncle Josh called me at some point, maybe an hour or two after I got to work. He asked me where I was.

"I'm at work. Why?"

"Okay. Stay there." And he hung up.

It was coming. It was on top of me then. I kept trying to tend to the children, but I was too distracted to do anything more than go through the motions.

My dad called about twenty minutes later, telling me to pack up my niece, then go over to my brother's middle school to pick him up, then get home.

"If your boss gives you a hard time, just tell her it's a family emergency."

When he said that, I actually had a moment of hope. To me, "family emergency" was more of a term people would use if someone was injured, but alive. Not in good condition, maybe, but alive.

Still, I didn't ask for clarification.

I hurried to pack the baby's things, then realized that I didn't have a car seat for her. After a frantic back-and-forth texting session with my parents, trying to figure out how we were going to get her home, we finally decided to let her stay at the daycare center for a little longer. It was either that, or put her in a car with no car seat, and that was not going to happen.

After I calmed down from the frustration of it all, I gave her a hug and a kiss and took off for my brother's school, about ten minutes away.

The receptionist gave me a hard time about pulling my brother out of the school, telling me I wasn't authorized to do so. I told her to get him *now*. She did.

He was confused, asking me what was going on, why I'd come to get him and what was happening at home. All I could manage was to tell him it was bad, a family emergency.

When we got home, there was a weird, silent, stressed-out feeling in our house. No one was really saying anything. So I did what I always do when I'm tense: I started cleaning things.

Around ten o'clock, I was folding laundry when the first police officer showed up at our door. My little brother suddenly started hugging me as the officer came in, and I snapped, "Why are the police here? *Why*?"

But I knew why. I just didn't *want* to know why, but he was going to tell me and it made me angry.

Then Mommy and Daddy pulled us into their arms as he told us.

My brother broke away and ran upstairs to his room. I felt my stomach turning over as I hurried to the bathroom, where I vomited for at least half an hour.

When I came out, I heard my mother scream, "He *shot* her? He shot *Emali*?"

I didn't want to hear the rest. I couldn't. I left to call my boyfriend.

My memories of the rest of that day come back to me in pieces, just scattered moments that are hard to put in order, so I don't really try. Maybe I will later on in my life. Just not now.

I GUESS I'M ADAPTING to life without Emali, but I sometimes think that I'm not doing a good job with that. Too many areas of my life have gone kind of gray. I just feel like the volume in which I once lived my life has been turned way down, like all the things I valued, enjoyed, or worried about are moot when compared to April 10th, 2024.

The one area where I know I'm struggling is also the most important one: My faith. I try to stay interested in church, I try to read my Bible, I try to pray - but there's an emptiness inside me that I can't seem to fill.

As much as I miss my sister, I also miss the family we used to be. We were loud, and goofy, and always busy; yet somehow, we made time to be together and enjoy our lives with each other. Now we've been forced to rebuild without a vital part of what we once had, and we don't know how to do that. At least, not yet.

I wonder what created this situation. I try to figure out how someone gets to the point of killing his child's mother, but I have no answers. If anything, all I wind up with are more questions.

Maybe there are lapses in parental involvement with these guys - not only with both parents in the home, but what if one parent is missing from the picture? Do these boys who grow up to be abusive men have histories of watching and learning from an abusive male figure in their lives? Is it some kind of deep-seated insecurity that makes them latch on to their victim, then decide to destroy her if she tries to leave? Are their minds ruined by drugs?

I'm pretty sure that they're not held accountable for what they do wrong, or they would learn some kind of respect for others. Either that, or they just can't be taught, which I have to think would make them plenty scary to their *own* families as they get older and bigger.

I don't know. It probably wouldn't make me feel that much better if I did know, but I do think we need to study these guys and find the answers we need. More than that, we need to make sure that the people around them are safe.

I will always believe that Emali and her little girl deserve nothing less.

Heidi

"I want to always remember the laughter."

IN MY QUIET MOMENTS, I close my eyes and bring up my memories of Emali. You know those family stories that seem to pop up around the holiday table every year? So many of ours revolve around her.

When she and her sister were little, Emali would always make Eva do things first. Swimming, sledding down a big hill, taking the training wheels off the bike - Eva would try everything out first. I never figured out if Emali followed her because she was really smart, or if she was just very cautious. I think it was probably both.

There are so many beautiful moments from her life that suddenly come back to me, especially when I'm with my granddaughter. Emali was a very young mother, some would say too young, but she was absolutely amazing. She was very involved and responsible, and she adored her baby. There were times when she would be working, and she would text me constant reminders about how to take care of the baby, until I would finally respond with something like, "Keep in mind that I raised *you*, so have a seat. I know what I'm doing." She was in the process of creating her own memories with her child, so she hated missing even a moment with her. I know exactly how she felt.

One of my favorite memories is when Emali was three years old, and we took her to a place where she could feed animals. She was trying to feed a donkey a carrot, but she didn't let go of it in time, and the donkey pretty much swallowed her entire hand. I had to hurry to pull it out. She didn't seem all that upset about it, which I suppose is the reason we can laugh at it.

We laughed a lot. Emali was so entertaining when she laughed - it was like it took over her entire body, and she would become almost immobile.

That's what I want to remember. More than anything else, I want to always remember the laughter.

Kyra
Emali's best friend

"There's an empty seat beside me."

EMALI'S MURDER TURNED my life inside-out.

I loved her. She was a great daughter, a great mom, and a great friend. I miss her more than I'll ever be able to describe to anyone.

In early March of 2024, Emali invited me over to her place to talk about her relationship with her daughter's father. She told me then that she was done with him. She said he was smoking pot, not working, and basically just bedrotting. She had decided that she was going to leave him and go back home to her mom's house.

"You've tried your best with him," I said. "You have to do what's best for you and your daughter." I offered to help in whatever way I could, with whatever she needed, and gave her my work schedule in case she wanted to plan around that.

I got a text from Emali the next day. She said that her boyfriend was angry, accusing her of giving up too easily. She seemed to be wavering with her decision to leave.

"You've tried your best," I said again. "You have to take care of yourself and the baby."

She didn't leave at that time. I was a little surprised, but back then, I didn't know about the abuse. Emali never told me. No one else who might have known had mentioned it to me, either. I wish I'd known - my response would have been much more than it was then. The very least I would have done would have been to go straight to her family and start sounding the alarms.

On April 10th, around 9:30 p.m., Heidi messaged me to ask if I'd heard from Emali that evening. I told her I hadn't, so we spent some time going back and forth, trying to come up with logical reasons that Emali might be out of contact with us.

"But I have the baby here with me," she explained, "and she hasn't answered me since around four o'clock this afternoon."

"That's strange."

"I know. She hasn't checked on the baby at all."

It took a few seconds, but her comments hit me hard. That was completely out of character for Emali.

I said, "She might be sleeping. Maybe she got tired from all the packing?"

"But she never even let me know she wouldn't be coming back tonight."

Again, I tensed up. Emali didn't do stuff like that, just take off and tell no one - especially since she'd had her daughter.

"Do you know if they got into a fight or something? Did they break up?"

Heidi told me that they had, but only briefly, and then got back together. Emali hadn't mentioned that to me at all. To this day, I still wonder why. Maybe she thought I would try to stop her from going back to her boyfriend. She would have been right.

When I asked Heidi what Emali had been saying about him, she told me he kept asking what he could do to fix things between them. It sounded like he just kept trying to wear Emali down with his persistence - but this time, she was actually done with him. She was leaving.

I couldn't think of any other reassuring reasons that Emali had suddenly gone silent, so I offered to go to the house Emali shared with her boyfriend and see if she was there, and Heidi gratefully accepted the offer.

I got to Emali's place sometime around ten or ten-thirty on the night of April 10th. As I pulled up to the driveway, I took note of the fact that both her car and his were in the driveway. I had this painful sinking sensation in my stomach, sort of like I was afraid, but more like I was just filled with dread.

I went to the front door and knocked, then listened closely for any activity inside. There was none. I knocked again, harder this time, and waited - still nothing. Then I pounded on the door as hard as I could. When no one answered that time, I tried to open the door, but it was locked. I shielded my eyes against the front door's window and looked inside as best I could, but couldn't really see anything.

I went back to my car and called Heidi, told her how the lights were on and the curtains were drawn - which was also unusual - but no one was answering the locked front door.

She asked, "Do you feel like something's wrong?"

"Yeah. I do. Do you think I should call the police?"

"Yes. Call the police."

It took a couple of tries to actually reach the correct police department, because I was initially put through to the wrong one; but when I finally reached Minot police, I asked them for a welfare check. They couldn't tell me how long it would take to get a patrol car out there, but I did wait for a while before I headed for home. I didn't know what else to do.

The police officer who wound up going to the house was nice enough to update me a few times about what was going on, which was something I really appreciated. I couldn't sleep anyway.

Around two a.m., he called me and told me they'd gone to the house and pounded on the door for a while, but there was no answer. Since it was what they called "sleeping hours," and this was a welfare check - which I'm assuming is a different procedure from a complaint - they couldn't force entry at that point. He promised that they would return to the house as early as possible in the morning, and that he would keep me informed.

I finally fell asleep around three o'clock. When I woke up around 10:30 that morning, I immediately texted Heidi and asked if there was any news. She called me a few minutes later.

"Have you heard from her?"

"Kyra," she paused, and it seemed like an hour went by before she said, "she's gone."

Hearing those words... How do you describe it to someone? It's like your brain short-circuits or something. All I could do was cry. And I did that for hours. I couldn't stop. The entire time that we all waited to hear, I'd had a feeling that he'd killed Emali; yet when Heidi actually said it, it still shocked me.

Emali was my best friend, but she was also a friend to everyone who knew her. That was one of the most beautiful things about her - the way that she truly cared for and about people. While I have specific memories of fun times and happy moments, what I miss the most is having her in my life. The totality of having her as a huge part of my life. That's what I miss the most.

We used to take off on late-night drives, listening to music and talking, just enjoying being young. Every so often, I'll go for a drive and turn up the music, but it's not the same. There's an empty seat beside me. And no one will ever be able to fill that empty space.

IN THE WEEKS THAT FOLLOWED Emali's death, I pretty much dropped out of life. I pulled away or even gave up on most things and just kept to myself. My schoolwork suffered quite a bit, but I did manage to keep my job.

The worst of my grieving took several weeks, during which I merely existed. I feel like I'm slowly coming back, but there are aftereffects - like how I can't sleep by myself anymore without having the kind of dreams that haunt you the next day. I have dreams of Emali still being here, and I'll wake up sobbing, wanting her to come back. Those are becoming less frequent, though.

I'm trying to find ways to rejoin the world, but it doesn't help that every day, I ask myself why this happened. Why did he kill her? Was it just to make sure that no one else would ever have her?

I keep remembering the time when Emali first met him. He was so quiet, which made me think he was just shy. The serious type. He just didn't speak much, didn't seem to let anyone in. I've since learned that the difference between quietly shy and oppressively silent can be figured out if you look closely, and that difference can be huge. It can be the biggest thing in the world, a symptom of the beginning of a tragedy.

He didn't seem to want to know any of Emali's friends. He certainly didn't want to be around us; and to me, that's now the initial red flag that I missed, so I never suspected the abuse I've heard about since he killed Emali. But now, I see him through the lens of being the guy who shot my best friend because she tried to get away. The way I see it, she wanted to live her life on her terms, so he killed her. I mean, how do you process that? And how did he become the person who would do that?

I don't know. I'll probably never know. This kind of thing happens often enough that you'd think we would have some answers, yet here we are. We can throw around ideas about culture, and norms, and upbringing. We talk about the possibility that drug usage might be a factor. But the one thing I keep going back to is that in my opinion, when women are murdered by an intimate partner, it's likely that someone, *somewhere* in his world had an idea about the dangers he presented. If the people around him don't help, well, I have a problem with that. At least they should try to *get* him help. Or maybe at least warn the women who might become victims.

I know, that's probably not realistic. After all, it's possible that others in his world are intimidated by him.

I wish Emali had told me. I hope that battered women will read this, then take a hard look at their lives, and then ask themselves *why* they're keeping his secrets. I hope they tell someone, lots of people, especially everyone who loves them - so those people won't have to stare at an empty seat for the rest of their lives.

Becca

"What happened to Emali will not be forgotten."

THIS IS THE EULOGY I wrote for Emali. I didn't present it because I just couldn't on that day, but I'd like to share it here.

I WANT TO START OUT by saying that the turnout today shows how loved Emali was. Most people describe her as vibrant, beautiful, funny - any of the things you would typically say about a person like Emali.

While all of those things are true, the best thing Emali ever did was be a mom.

Everyone in this room knows what it was like to be loved by Emali. She was kind, caring, had a very dark sense of humor - just like her mom - but she was also one of the best damn moms you'll ever meet. The best, actually.

Her little girl was truly her pride and joy. Everyone always says moms would do anything for their kids. That was so true with Emali. Being so young, people doubted her, but she would move Heaven and Earth for that baby to be happy. Whether that was driving to Nonna's house at 8:00 at night because the baby just wanted to see her Nonna, or picking her up at every request even when her arms were about ready to fall off, Emali's daughter came first in every situation - even when that meant Emali had

36

to come last. She cared so deeply about her residents, her little brother and sister, her whole family. But most of all, she loved her child.

Emali was a ray of sunshine in every room she walked into. It didn't matter if it was a Monday morning when you were dragging your butt into work, she somehow made the day better. Some of my own favorite memories were working with Emali. When something happened at work, her immediate response was, "I'm going to go call my mommy."

She was obsessed with her mom. She never called her "Mom," though. She always called her "Mommy." I can't remember a single night when Heidi and I hung out where Emali didn't call just to talk about her day, and every time the phone rang, we knew it was going to be at least a half-hour conversation. At the time, Heidi and I would smile and roll our eyes, because this happened all the time and no one thought it would ever stop.

I know, sitting here today, that Heidi would give anything for another one of those phone calls.

I wish I wasn't talking about Emali in the past tense. She should be here today. Her daughter deserved to know her mother, more than just in pictures and videos. She was taken far too soon and completely unjustly, but everyone in this room knows that she fought her hardest, even in her last few moments.

Domestic Violence is real. It's not a joke. Emali's story will not be forgotten, and I hope everyone in this room makes sure that's the case. Please continue to support the family in fighting the fight against Domestic Violence in the years to come so Emali's story is not forgotten.

And to Emali's family: Today is going to be the longest and hardest day of your lives. Just know that everyone here loved Emali so much, and will continue to love and support you as much as they can. None of you deserved any of this, and I'm so sorry this happened. We will continue to raise awareness about Domestic Violence.

What happened to Emali will not be forgotten.

Heidi

Of all the things I miss, I miss her phone calls the most.

Emali had such precise timing when it came to those phone calls. I hated waking up at 5.30, 6 o'clock in the morning to my phone ringing, but the most annoying ones were when I was home from work and exhausted, all settled into my bed for a quick nap, and my phone would announce that Renee - which is what I called her - was Facetiming me. Without fail, it happened just as I was drifting off to sleep.

She would want to talk sometimes about important things, because she wanted to hear my perspective - just to help her make a decision. Sometimes she called because of simple boredom. She just wanted to have somebody on the phone. It was nice being her go-to somebody.

I never made her feel like an imposition, which is why these calls went on for so many years, but I have to admit that there were times I had to sigh deeply before answering. As you can imagine, I'd give anything to get one more call, one more silly conversation, one more request for advice.

There are times when I'm going through my day and something happens that I want to share with Emali, and I have that impulse to call her. The pain in my heart as I realize I will never again talk to her... I can't begin to describe it.

But if I could, I would tell her again how proud I am of her. I would make sure she knew that I will always love her endlessly. I think she knew that. I hope she did.

And I would tell her to call me any time.

"Anna"
Former target of Domestic Violence

"Try to open your minds to an alternate reality that battered women know all too well."
("Anna" is an assumed name for the woman interviewed here, and is intended to protect her identity. Her story is real.)

I'M FAMILIAR WITH THE story of Emali Sallee. I think we're all familiar with at least some of these hideous events, most of which occur because too many people are *not* familiar with the reality of abuse. They don't know what it is to live your life with the abuser.

It isn't a series of events, not at all. Domestic Violence is a perpetual crime. It's a lifestyle. It's an oppressive force that swallows up every waking moment, casting a shadow over a woman's life. Be it from fear, outrage, protecting the children, recovering from the injuries, constantly putting up a front and/or outright lying to others, or manipulation of the batterer to keep him placated - which any battered woman will tell you is just a temporary respite - the life of an abused woman is spent trying desperately to prevent the inevitable. He's going to explode again at some point. The question we live with isn't so much, "When?" It's "How bad will it be?"

So naturally, that brings us to the eternal, damning question: "If he was so awful, why didn't you just *leave*?"

I'll speak only for myself here, although I do know of many other stories, mostly through support groups I attended. Many of us had the same reasons for staying as long as we did.

My now ex-husband and I had a daughter together. While some of you reading this are succumbing to a hissy fit over that, appalled that I would "allow" my child to remain in an abusive household, try to open your minds to an alternate reality that battered women know all too well: Separation and divorce lead to visitation, usually unsupervised - because in keeping the truth of my relationship a secret, the ex had no black marks on his life.

And why did I keep it a secret? First, because I was at a supreme disadvantage financially. He reminded me on a regular basis that I had no income (the one time I went out and got a job, I wound up with a concussion and a broken wrist), and that he could "buy and sell me" on a whim. One of his favorite threats was that if I ever tried to leave, he would get a lawyer who would not only take my daughter from me, but who would also bury me financially. He controlled the finances and often used them as discipline.

Second, with all of that being the case, I knew better than to tarnish his façade of a happy family. Everyone thought he was a great guy. A good provider. A family man. The rare times I tried to talk about my situation with friends, they flat-out didn't believe me. One even asked what I did to make him so angry. And I actually spent some time trying to figure out an answer to that question.

And finally, taking my story to the police or social workers would have put me in the position of either being accused of failing to protect my daughter, or turning her over to him for the afore-mentioned unsupervised visitation. No way was I going to leave her alone with a guy who called her "a little bitch" who was "just like her mother."

I recorded him saying those things, and much worse, and then took advantage of free consultations with family law lawyers on three separate occasions. They all cautioned me that the judges whom they appeared in front of would frown on my recording him, that it would be seen as "self serving" and "manipulative." I learned that a mother who fails to hide the truth about the batterer from the children is often cited for being an alienator, and that label often leads to the mother losing custody.

The fact that my ex actually *said* all those things seemed lost within my apparent moral failing of first, not being able to hide everything from my daughter and second, then taking the measures to prove what he was doing. The lawyers said that the way the court saw it, he wasn't responsible for the fact that my daughter was terrified of him. *I* was to blame, because I didn't adequately conceal his abuse.

I look back on that time now, and I thank God that I managed to keep my wits about me enough to get my daughter and myself out of there alive. The gaslighting done by an abuser is devastating, designed to keep his victim confused and off-balance, and there were times when he succeeded in doing that to me. The most galling thing my ex did was to do something horrible, then stare me straight in the eyes and insist that *I* did it. And I would have this moment of doubt, especially in the early years, that made me less likely to fight back. It soon became the norm.

The lawyers I consulted with all said that by the age of fourteen, most family courts would let my daughter decide where she wanted to live, or at least allow her to have a decent amount of input. One month before her fourteenth birthday, with the help of a dear friend who - through experiences of her own - finally believed me, my daughter and I moved into our own apartment.

The ex made a lot of threats afterwards; but when it became clear to him that I wouldn't be coming back and I *would* get a restraining order, which was now a much safer thing to do since I was in my own home at that point, he backed down some. It would create a bad image for him, after all. And when he understood that in a courtroom, I'd have a chance to speak as well, he decided it wasn't worth having it all on the public record. We settled our matters and life finally began anew.

I'm sure that there are people out there who would still insist that I could have left anyway, and left earlier. And if I'm going to be fair, I would have been one of those misguided, uninformed people in the years before my marriage.

But there was another reason that I stayed, and that was my knowledge that if I tried to leave, he would kill me. And I didn't want to die. I firmly believe that when women know that threat is there, absolutely no one else has the right to contest it.

And no, I never told anyone about that fear, not while I was still in his house; after all, our social circle was a bunch of people who truly believed the lies he told about me. They seemed to believe that he was nothing less than heroic for putting up with me. He would tell them that I was unstable, bipolar, and abusive. That I was a horrible mother, completely inattentive and even neglectful towards my daughter. I personally overheard him tell some of his stories, and some were relayed to me by the woman who helped my daughter and me escape. Still others were shared with me by one of his friends who eventually saw the light, and the rest of the information came from what we battered mothers call the "flying monkeys": Ignorant bystanders who mindlessly chose to believe him and do his bidding. They, through their disappointed and sometimes contemptuous comments, helped him to keep me quiet.

What I find fascinating and very telling is this: Not one of those people ever asked *him*, "If she's so awful, why don't you just leave?"

I don't like to reveal what I'm about to talk about, because it makes me feel weak and stupid. I worry about coming across as defensive, which I suppose I am.

But it is another truth and I want to say it: In the early years with him, I loved him completely. He acted like he was kind, attentive, and faithful. We'd planned our lives together. I meant the vows I recited at our wedding, wearing my white gown and daydreaming about the beautiful future that was waiting for us. He was someone I totally trusted, enough that I had his child.

By the way, I think that people on the outside of an abused woman's life - maybe people in general - don't give any thought to the amount of trust a woman shows when she bears a man's child.

After I became pregnant, he started showing who he really was. What I'd like to get across here is how *heartbreaking* it is when that betrayal happens, and that it's tough to extricate yourself from the morass that should have been your marriage, at least until he's destroyed the love you once had for him. By that time, you're pretty well trapped.

I remember all of the moments that created my total disgust for him, but I'll share just the first one:

I was about four months along, starting to show, and I was pretty sure I was having a girl. On a whim, I went to a local store and bought a lacy pink infant's headband. I was excited for him to get home from work so I could show it to him. He'd been quiet for a couple of weeks, standoffish, which he attributed to stress at work. I was trying to make him feel better, maybe get him interested in the baby.

I made his favorite dinner, set a lovely table, and greeted him at the door with a hug that he pulled away from kind of roughly. When we sat down to eat, I showed him the headband. His expression went cold and he said, "You're that sure you're having a girl? You're sure enough to spend money on useless crap like that?"

I hadn't been let in on the rules of engagement at that point, so I snapped, "Don't talk to me like that."

His expression instantly turned to rage. He picked up his full plate, threw it like a Frisbee across the table at me, told me to go to hell, and stormed out. He slammed the front door hard enough that it cracked the casing and knocked our wedding portrait off the wall. He was gone for the next two days with no contact whatsoever.

I was a nervous wreck by the time he finally came home, which started creating this strange emotional fragility in me and went a long way toward teaching me how to be a doormat.

Instead of confronting the truth about the kind of guy who would behave as he did, I tried to prevent that type of incident from ever happening again.

But my heart was breaking. I *loved* him. I missed the man I thought I married. I wanted him to go back to being who he was on our wedding day. I was deluded enough to believe I had some sort of power over that, some kind of influence over his decisions. If, as he insisted, I could "make" him behave badly, then it follows that I could "make" him love me and our child. See the logic?

I believe that's the lie a lot of women fall into. They buy the rhetoric that says they're all-powerful in a man's life, so much so that they can make him a monster - yet for some unknown reason, their power ends there.

So how do women like me wind up with these guys?

I think batterers intuitively sense in others what they, themselves lack within their own souls, and they're able to manipulate their partners into a trap. Once they feel secure in their ability to control, they start to reveal who they really are, as long as they can twist it enough to blame it all on the woman they're abusing. I know that's a pretty general description, but I think it's accurate.

There's one more thing the abusers find very useful, and that's the ignorance and indifference, not to mention the judgmental attitudes, of people who have no idea what they're talking about. What do they care? They aren't the ones whose lives are being ripped apart. They can stand on the sidelines and criticize and critique, then play judge and jury against women and children who are in very real trouble. Then they can go home and think nothing of the fact that they're actually encouraging a monster to be monstrous - toward someone *else*.

I had many of those flying monkeys around me before I left my husband, and they were immeasurably destructive to my life. At times, they even created dangerous situations. Once I left, I had no contact whatsoever with them.

I also rid my life of the spectators who chose to remain blandly neutral. I seriously doubt that I will ever allow them into my life again. The only people I have greater contempt for are the ones who stay completely and contentedly blind to the truth, then have the unmitigated gall to judge the lives of women who are suffering. As angry as I am and will always be, I dearly hope that those people never have *any* reason to join our ranks. Like I said, I used to be one of the judgmental types, and I wouldn't wish the life that became my comeuppance on anyone.

With that, I send my deepest and most heartfelt condolences to Emali Sallee's loved ones. I'm *so* sorry for your loss. I hope you're all getting the loving and compassionate support that you need and deserve, and that my story causes at least some people to rethink their stance on the lunacy that took your beloved Emali from you. You all will remain in my thoughts.

Isaac
Emali's friend

"I try not to think about what might have been."

EMALI AND I WERE CLOSE friends.

I knew Emali since we were kids, for probably around eight years. We met through mutual friends at the Bangor State Fair, and ever since then, we had always been close. Our friendship was on again, off again at times when we were younger; but as we grew up, she became a very important person in my life.

She came up for a visit the weekend before she was killed. Watching her finally have the chance to have fun - to get away from the lockdown she had been in for so long - was probably the best time we'd ever had together. I loved watching her calling and texting to check on her daughter, which she did several times a day, because she was just this amazing mother and it was a beautiful thing to see.

That was one of the many things that was so special about her. Emali was one of the best mothers I ever saw. Sure, she was young when she had her baby, but that woman would have plowed through, knocked over, or burned down anything that stood between her and her child. She made sure her baby was loved, cared for, and protected.

Becoming a mother changed something within her: She was deeper, more thoughtful about everything in her life that might impact her child. Like I said, it was a beautiful thing to see, and it's one of the things I miss the most.

While Emali was always the one person who could brighten your day, she was also a true friend in the sense that she was honest. She said what she thought. She was firm in her convictions, yet she would also go out of her way to make sure everyone around her was heard, happy, and had whatever they needed. I suppose that in some ways, she was complicated - I mean, we all are, right? - but the true gift I got from knowing her was that I once had a friend who was a genuine person. No faking any part of her life, if you know what I mean. I haven't known many people like that, and I doubt I ever will.

I learned in the early morning hours of April 11th that no one had heard from Emali since the day before. I remember that sinking, hollow feeling in my gut when I found out.

Later that day, her sister Eva called me to let me know what had happened. That call broke something inside me, and I know it will never be put back together again.

I have trouble talking about that day any more specifically than that.

I'M SORT OF REBUILDING my life at this point, and I do function well enough; however, I still have so many questions that no one can answer for me. The one that haunts me the most is, why did this guy have to take away this truly amazing woman - the fantastic young mother, loving daughter to her parents, great sister, everyone's friend. *My* friend, the one who was always there for me. *Why?*

I want to know what causes a man to do this. Where do these guys come from? How do you get to the point of murdering a young woman who was just trying to live her life? This one heartless, hideous act has broken the hearts of everyone who loved Emali. He took a little piece of all of us with him. For some of us, he took more than a little.

Domestic Violence needs to be taken more seriously than it is at this time. There needs to be severe penalties for being convicted of DV. And I think that women need to feel safe telling people what is happening to them. I hope that what happened to Emali will encourage others who are being abused to *tell someone*.

Get help. People do care.

Emali was beautiful, brilliant, loving, sweet, funny... I'll never forget her. Of course I won't. I just feel like I was cheated, like we all were cheated - like Emali's life made such a wonderful impact on the world, and we didn't get nearly enough time with her. It's so unfair. I try not to think about what might have been, because there's nothing in the world that is as sad as that thought.

But I think about it anyway.

Emali will always be one of the most important people in my life. I hope she's able to rest in peace. I'll miss her forever.

Heidi

"I had a sick feeling in my gut that a battle was forming."

FROM MY INITIAL INTERACTION with him, I didn't like Emali's boyfriend.

My first impression of him just made me uneasy. Emali told me that she wanted to hang out with him. Since she was too young to be able to drive, I drove her over to his house. Besides, I wanted to make sure that one of his parents was home.

I asked to meet his mother, and she came out onto the porch where we introduced ourselves. It went okay, except for the fact that the boy didn't say anything to me. He just stood there staring at me.

Emali had told me that they were going to an apple orchard; however, when I later checked her location, they were still at his house. I texted her to find out why, but I thought her answer was somewhat lame, so I Facetimed her and told her that she needed to come home. Either I would pick her up or he could bring her back, but she was coming home.

It turned out that he was listening, which I suspected made him upset, because he simply dropped her off at the end of my driveway and took off. I had been stressing some over his attitude already, but that moment made my stomach clench. I felt that there was something truly off about the guy.

I asked, "Where did he go? Why did he drop you off like that?"

She answered with, "I don't know." She paused, then added, "Because I asked him to."

The way that she responded to me, I knew that she absolutely did *not* ask him to drop her off that way. She was covering up for him already, and I didn't like that.

With Emali already in her teens, I knew there would be times of her rebelling. There would be issues to deal with that I'd never before confronted. She would want more freedom, more autonomy, more privacy - and I didn't know where the lines would be drawn or how I would handle them.

Only a few years earlier, she was a little girl playing with her toys; now, everything was changing. I dreaded the thoughts I had of the fights that would eventually arrive in our lives.

At the same time, I had a sick feeling in my gut that a major battle was already being formed.

"Jordan"
Former Domestic Violence Advocate

("Jordan" is an assumed name for the person interviewed here, and is intended to protect their identity.)

I'M SO VERY SORRY FOR the family, the friends, the loved ones who will now live the rest of their lives without Emali. I think of you all every day.

I made a massive mistake in my preparation for contributing to this book. I did some research on the murder of Emali Sallee, wound up on a certain social media site, and then - and here's the beginning of the blunder - I read the comments.

Most were condolences, prayers, and words of encouragement; however, there were a fair amount of comments about the alleged failures of the murder victim's *mother*, an occurrence which was actually not at all shocking. To be honest, I fully expected it. I've seen it countless times. So what was the big mistake?

It was in my thinking that I'd be able to deal with it dispassionately.

I've been invited to be open and honest about my views in my contribution to this book; and while I'm somewhat uncomfortable with doing that - advocates are trained to be calm and reassuring, after all - I am going to try to lose the filter and speak my mind.

I spent many years working with women who were victims of Domestic Violence, so my perspective for this book comes from their experiences.

The one aspect of DV that I'll probably never fully understand is the contempt that battered women receive from certain segments of society. I refer to those people as "perch sitters." They're the kind who, seated safely above the fray, like to look down on others and blame them for the crimes being committed against them. I've often felt that they get a sense of security, maybe even superiority from denigrating oppressed women. Or maybe they're just afraid that it could happen to them, as well, so that's their method of denial? I don't know.

But in discussing abuse, it's important to mention these people - because they're part of the problem. I believe that in any injustice, those who attack the victims are more than cruel: They're actually allies of the criminal. And in this case, any indication that the mother of the murder victim bears any responsibility for the loss of her child is an indescribable cruelty. I also fear that it serves only to encourage more tragedies like the loss of Emali.

I won't go into detail about the content of the atrocious comments I've read, because I don't want them to see any more daylight and I want to move on to other topics; however, I do sincerely hope that the people spewing such hatred never have reason to eat their words.

IT'S IRONIC TO ME THAT I seem to comprehend the abuser's mindset more and better than I understand the perch sitters. I think that's because batterers tend to have extraordinarily similar ways of thinking. When you talk with them, which I've done quite often in my work, they tend to say the same things about themselves, their partners, and even the culture as a whole. Many of them believe that society is inherently unfair to men, and they behave as they do because *they* are the ones being oppressed. It's *others* who are causing them to be violent; and almost always, the "bad" person at the top of their list is their victim. That's why it's so dangerous when people sympathize with abusers. Doing so reinforces their mindset that they're not responsible for their actions - that they can be pushed into being violent.

I'd like to see more effort put into studying batterers, and less energy spent on psychoanalyzing the women they abuse. Why do we continually speculate on her reasons for staying instead of his reasons for hurting her? Or how she might provoke him to violence, instead of the fact that he's able to be provoked to that extent? Why do we pay attention to, even *support* his excuses about having his buttons pushed, yet give no thought to the idea that she has buttons, as well?

I guess my bottom-line question is, why are we putting the victim on the defensive instead of the criminal?

I was going to comment here anyway on the reasons women stay with abusers, but to be honest, I've grown weary of explaining those dynamics. I firmly believe that people who take even a *few* moments to stop castigating women, and start thinking about it logically, will figure it all out just fine.

Besides, since you're reading this book about the murder of Emali Sallee, I hope you understand that you're already up to speed on Reason One.

And seeing as I've already said all I care to about the abuser, there's just one more facet of this issue that I want to address - and that's all about you.

First, don't accept as a goal the utopian ideal that we will ever rid our society of all abusers. It sounds good, and it makes people feel good, but there will never be a time where Domestic Violence ceases to occur. For as long as human beings have free will, there will always be controlling, angry, self-entitled types who regard themselves as the put-upon victims of others - and who firmly believe that these "others" give them no alternative but to be violent. However, there is much that can be done to minimize the batterer's ability to destroy lives.

For example, don't wait until DV appears at your own front door before you decide to get involved. Whether it's aimed directly at you, or a loved one is being abused, it's usually too late to affect the outcome once you wake up to it. Besides, with the current prevalence of DV, chances are that the crime of Domestic Violence is *already* affecting your life, even if there's no active abuser in your midst.

Let's explore that. Beyond the economic impact, which some estimates place in the tens of billions of dollars annually and is stunning in its scope, let's just talk about your own day-to-day existence, lived within what you believe is an abuse-free environment.

The screaming road-rager who cut you off on your drive to work - what's his issue? What about the kid at your child's school who bullies his classmates. He's witnessing that behavior somewhere, right? The coworker who always calls out at the last minute might be at the E.R. getting help for her injuries, or maybe she's just hiding them at home. The cashier who screwed up your order - is she having trouble concentrating? What about the woman next door who wears long sleeves on a ninety-degree day? Or the friend who scares so easily that you make sure you never startle her - is she hiding something?

Speculation? Sure. And perhaps none of those examples affect you in the least. How's about the fact that being beaten and oppressed by a batterer creates an increased risk of substance abuse? Could drug users have an impact on your life?

Again, maybe not. Hard to imagine that it doesn't, but okay.

If you know someone who is becoming increasingly withdrawn, depressed, and isolated, is it possible that she's hiding the fact that she's being abused? Do you have a friend or acquaintance who constantly cancels plans at the last minute?

Think about the rude, even nasty woman at the table next to you in the restaurant. These days, we call her "Karen," blast her on social media, then sit back and laugh at her. I suppose some would insist that Karens deserve such treatment, but what if the Karen at the next table has had the humanity beaten out of her very soul?

Do you have children? The kids who are growing up in an abuser's home, learning the value of women at the hands of a violent man, are going to be the adults who will one day show up for *your* daughter.

Now if you're sufficiently insulated from life, have no children whom you care about, and don't really worry about others anyway, then none of what I've said will affect you and the points are moot.

So let's try this instead: That constantly-fighting couple next door finally separates. He comes after her with his 9mm - and you happen to be in the line of fire. Or he comes into your workplace with a rifle, ready to take his revenge. Those scenarios might affect you. It *has* happened to others.

The point is, a third of the women you'll see today are being or have been abused. That's the commonly referenced stat, reflecting *reported* cases, so you need to accept that it's pretty much all around you.

With that said, the reason I gave you all those examples of what the results of abuse so often look like is actually very simple: I want you to be on the lookout for signs among the women and children whom you have in your life. I want you to be aware. I want you to be absolutely vigilant, and if you see the symptoms, I want you to help them. Get involved. Find a way. Don't back down in the face of a minimizing culture that for some reason regards a battered woman as less-than, just because the guy who beats her was once a man she loved and trusted. If you saw a woman being mugged on the street, would you walk away, blaming her for pushing the thief's buttons - or would you intervene?

The mode and method of helping will vary depending on the person and the situation, and of course, you need to educate yourself on the best practices for how to *safely* help; but if the victim knows that you know, and you handle the problem with appropriate care and concern - with *all* of your support going to the victim - the very least you'll accomplish is that the violence will come out of the shadows, which is exactly where it thrives.

Personally, I'd like to see more attention and resources given to advocacy that exposes more of the truth about *batterers*, as opposed to facts about domestic violence. I'd like us to work more on stopping them instead of studying them.

I don't have rose-colored glasses on. There are instances, like Emali's, that are especially difficult. A legal adult who is still a teenager is very hard to reach, which is why I felt I had to say something about the cruel comments on social media about Emali's mother. She did all she could to reach and to help her daughter, and was ultimately successful; however, when Emali decided to leave her boyfriend, she made the biggest mistake of all: She tried to do so with no backup. No protection. And this beautiful young mother is dead, her child is an orphan, and the family must now try to survive the most devastating thing that can happen to a loved one and those who were close to her.

Although it will be difficult for them to obtain, I wish them all a future of peace.

Heidi

MY LITTLE GIRL IS GONE.

My sweet, funny, beautiful little girl. The child with the biggest heart you'd ever come across, who loved her life and everyone in it - she's gone.

All day, every day, I have this straining, desperate need to somehow pull her back. I lay down to try to sleep at night, and the day always ends with the feeling of helpless frustration that comes from knowing that she's never coming back, and it's not fair. I wouldn't ever have been ready to lose her, but to have her ripped away before she had a chance to actually live her life... I don't know how to process that. I can't deal with any of it.

There are times when I feel like I'm clinging to Emali, trying to hang on to my happy memories of her and the family that we once were. Yet I can't stop reliving the day that I learned she was gone, and the hours leading up to it. I don't *want* to stop. Not yet. It's like if I relive it all, maybe I can rewrite the outcome. I can pull her away from the horror that was the end of her life, take her home, and keep her safe.

That's a big part of what haunts me: I didn't save her. I wasn't there to rescue her. At the moment when she needed me the most, I wasn't there.

I don't know how to navigate life without her. She was such a huge part of our lives, all of us - her family, her friends, the people who were fortunate enough to know her.

Raising Emali was simply a lot of fun. She had her difficult-to-manage attributes, like the fact that she was amazingly strong-willed. There was no way to move her off of her decisions. In some ways, her stubbornness was actually an asset in her life as a young mother, because she took full responsibility for her child. She made the decisions. Overall, her decisions as a mother were good ones. But I stayed close, worrying about her since she was so young; however, I was proud of how she cared for her child.

She was only 15 when she got pregnant, and 16 when her daughter was born. Emali's first challenge afterwards was that she had postpartum depression, but we got that taken care of, and she seemed to take to motherhood like a duck to water. Her baby was everything to her. Emali made sure that her daughter came first and that she was cared for consistently. If Emali wasn't on duty, it would be me. If Emali wanted to take a shower or grab a meal, she would ask her sister to watch the baby. It was a point of pride for me that my granddaughter was always so wonderfully taken care of.

During that difficult time of the PPD, I allowed her to drop out of high school to tend to her mental health. She returned to school relatively quickly, though, graduated early, and immediately went for her CNA license.

It was a good move. She absolutely loved her new career. Her boyfriend was still in the picture; but if I'm going to be honest, I had hoped that their relationship would end with her pregnancy. I wanted him to back out.

I say that because I was seeing signs of his abuse by then, and of course, I didn't want him around my daughter or my granddaughter.

I had suspected at least some type of emotional abuse for some time, because it seemed that he was always trying to control everything

Emali did. For example, we went to visit my ailing grandmother shortly after the baby was born. Her health was going downhill, so we wanted her to meet her great-great-granddaughter. He was messaging, texting, calling the entire time - angrily accusing Emali of things that she wasn't doing. She just wanted Gran to meet the baby.

A few weeks later, around the end of August, Emali had made plans to go to the beach with her friends and I volunteered to babysit. She wound up calling me from a number I didn't recognize. When I answered the phone, she said, "Mommy, it's Emali."

I asked her what phone she was calling from, and she said, "I borrowed a police officer's phone."

My stomach gripped, and I asked, "Why?"

"It's a long story. Can you come get me?"

Of course, I got there as fast as I could. She had bruises all over her legs and arms. I asked her what the hell *happened* to her, and she said that she'd made her plans to go to the beach with her friends, and her boyfriend had said it was fine - until she was getting ready to leave. Then he didn't want her to go.

She said that she told him she was going out anyway, to which he replied, "No, you *aren't* going." They argued until it escalated to the point that he wound up putting a pillow over her face and punching her arms and legs.

I asked her where her phone was. She said he grabbed it from her, threw it somewhere, then wouldn't let her take it with her when she left the house.

I said, "That's not his phone. And *you* are not his property. He doesn't have the right to tell you that you can't leave. You don't even live there." Their situation was that she had started staying there quite often, because with his controlling nature, it was too draining for her to stay elsewhere.

She used my phone to call his mother on the way home. In listening to the conversation Emali had with her, I learned that his mother knew he had put his hands on my daughter.

I was stunned. I took the phone away from Emali and I asked the woman what the hell she was *thinking*. The only response that she gave to me was that they were putting their hands on each other. It seemed she was regarding the assault as some kind of mutual combat.

I said, "Even if that *were* true, self defense isn't the same as putting your hands on each other. Either way, your son is three times the size of my daughter, and you just allowed that to happen."

She kept asking to talk to Emali, and I said, "No, you're not talking to Emali. You're talking to *me*. Emali is sixteen years old. You don't get to talk to her anymore. Now you're talking to me."

I don't recall ever, in my entire life, being that angry. I took Emali to the courthouse to try to get her to fill out a restraining order. She began filling out the paperwork, but she got upset and said, "Mommy, this doesn't feel right. It feels wrong. I shouldn't be doing this."

I answered with, "You need to be doing this. He put his hands on you. What happens if he gets mad at the baby when she gets older? This is something you *have* to do."

Still, she refused to talk to the judge. She said she just felt too bad about getting him into that kind of trouble. I wasn't buying that, not completely; more than once, she had shared with me how afraid she was to leave the baby alone with him, and of course he would at some point demand visitation if she left him. She needed to at least try to be on good terms with him.

So I contacted the police for a standby, went to his house, and helped her get all of her stuff out. While we were there, I asked the police officers, "Can I fill out a protection order - with her being sixteen and a minor - and keep her away from him?"

They said that I could do that. It was within my rights. However, if she decided to leave me and go back to his house, they wouldn't be able to hold him accountable for violating the restraining order.

Emali eventually reconciled with him, and they moved into his grandparents' trailer. They had recently passed away, the property was still in Probate Court, and I was told that the boyfriend's mother suggested that they move into the place together and keep an eye on it while it was making its way through the court system. When they first moved in, I would go over quite frequently. I'd bring dinner, or I'd bring the baby home to them and they'd put her to bed. Then I would leave so that she wouldn't freak out that I was leaving.

But then, for the final six months or so, every time I went there, she'd call me beforehand and ask me to bring something she needed. Often, it was food. And she would always meet me outside, even in the middle of winter or during bad weather. I kept asking her, "Why don't you want me to go inside your house?"

She always came back with, "Oh, it's just messy and I don't want to deal with it right now. It's just messy. I don't want to do it right now."

I think that she wasn't allowed to have me in the house. I think that he was telling her that he didn't want me there, but she still had to keep in contact with me to some degree because I'm her mom. Also, she depended on me to take care of her daughter.

But it seemed like he wouldn't let Emali go *anywhere*. He would be okay with her plans to see friends until she was about to leave the house, and then he would protest. Before the day he killed her, the most recent time this happened was when she made plans to go to the trampoline park with one of her friends. It was fine with him until that morning.

Emali planned on leaving at 12:30 so she could meet her friend at 1:00. Her boyfriend woke up at nine, and Emali reminded him that she was leaving in a few hours.

He told her that was fine - he just had to go to the store first, which meant he needed the one car they were sharing at the time. Ten o'clock came and went, but he still hadn't left, so she reminded him that she was leaving at 12:30. The same thing happened at eleven o'clock, and at noon, she told him that she was leaving in half an hour to meet her friend, so he'd better run his errand fast.

What followed was a huge fight, lots of yelling and screaming. Afterwards, Emali called me and asked me to come get the baby, because fighting that hard just for the right to leave the house was exhausting. She wanted to go to bed and rest.

What I finally saw, clearly now, was a guy who was wearing her down, isolating her, and using her child as a means of control, and I had reached the limit of my patience. I sat Emali down and explained my perspective in no uncertain terms. I told her he was narcissistic, abusive, and that she had no responsibility to continue to endure his behavior. This time, I seemed to reach her.

She said, "Yeah, I know, Mommy. And I want to get out. I want to leave. We can't stay in this house all the time. I look like an idiot because I'm making these plans with people, and then I have to turn around and make some crap excuse because I don't want to make myself look bad, but I don't want to make myself look *worse* by making it known that I'm being controlled by some dude. So I have to come up with some excuse. I have to lie to my friends and I just don't *like* it. I want to be able to go out and have fun. I want to watch my baby have fun and grow and make friends, and I can't."

Then she decided that she was going to take a few days away from him. She stayed with me for the weekend, had a friend whom she hadn't seen for a long time come over, and tried to relax. She needed space.

But he kept blowing up her phone. He managed to wear her down again, making promises about how he was going to finally get a job, things would be better, and so on. She ended up going back over there.

Of course the interviews, if they even actually happened, never resulted in a job. Nothing ever got better between them. Nothing changed at all.

It was on a Monday morning that Emali managed to get out of the house for a bit and called me. She was ready to make her plans to escape.

She said, "I have to work today and I have to work tomorrow, but I have Wednesday off. So on Wednesday, I'll take the baby to daycare and then I'll go back to the house. I'll pack up all our stuff and I will move home."

Emali and Eva were also talking to their father about staying at his rental house in Sabattus and paying him rent. That way, they would have their own place and they could live like adults, but still have their mom and dad as their cushion if they needed it. It was a good plan. It would have made sense.

Emali's father was okay with it as long Emali's boyfriend didn't live there. Their dad still had tenants in the house, so Emali was going to stay with me until the house was available for her and her sister.

For the first time in months, I was beginning to see a dim light at the end of the tunnel. Her relationship with him made me feel at times like I was walking an emotional tightrope - wanting to protect her, but having to always be careful to not drive her back to him.

On Wednesday morning, April tenth, she was supposed to be getting her stuff together, and then she was coming home. She simply wouldn't allow anyone to go with her to get her things. She didn't want to turn it into a huge drama, she said. She dropped the baby off at daycare and headed for their house in Minot, planning on finishing the packing and getting out of there in time to pick her daughter up. I was hoping that the time limit there, needing to go get the baby in time, would motivate Emali to get her things and leave quickly.

I was at work and in meetings when she started Facetiming me. When I answered and asked her what was going on, she asked if I could go to the daycare and get the baby.

My stomach dropped. "Honey, why can't you pick her up? What's going on?"

She said, "Mommy, it's just taking longer than I thought for me to get my stuff."

I could see her. She had the phone propped up and she was rapidly going through clothes in the living room and putting everything in bags. She was stressing. I could see it in her face and I could see it in her body language that she was starting to wear out, and I didn't want her to make the decision to give up.

"Okay, honey. Listen, I want you to relax and try to be calm. I want you to have as much time as you need because you're making the right decision. I'll figure it out. I can go get the baby and then I'll see you later. I'll see you when you get home."

"Okay, thank you so much, Mommy. That makes me feel so much better."

That was the last time I heard from her.

I COULDN'T LEAVE MY job until 5.15 that evening. My job is further away from daycare than my house, so Emali would always check on my location starting at 4:50 p.m. to see where I was at, to make sure I was on my way. If I hadn't left my house or left my job by five o'clock, she started texting me. So when it was a quarter after five and I didn't get a text message asking where I was, I thought that was a bit weird.

But then I was at a stoplight and I texted her. I said, "You have her bubby."

My granddaughter has to take a medication at night because she has an issue with her bowels. The only way to get the medication into her, and the only way for the medication to work, is to get it into her all at one time. At least six ounces of liquid just down the hatch. Getting a two year old to drink that much at one time is almost impossible.

So she still has a bubby – a bottle at night with milk with her medication, and I didn't have any more. When Emali left on Sunday, she took her daughter's last bubby with her. So I was at that stoplight and I texted her so that would remind her to grab it. With those types of things, I would always get an immediate response back.

Nothing came back. I thought that was very strange, because she would have checked my location and said something like, "Where are you? Why aren't you at daycare yet?" Because by this time it was 5:24.

When she didn't answer me when I asked her about the bubby, in my head, I was wondering, "What is she *doing*?"

I tried to come up with something other than the thought that was trying to form in the back of my mind. Maybe she was really busy getting her things out.

But she didn't ask me if I brushed the baby's teeth or not, she didn't ask me what time she went to bed, she didn't ask me to Facetime her before she went to sleep - all the things she did every single time I had the baby. Something was wrong.

And sitting at that stoplight, I started to get oddly emotional. I can't really explain it well - it was a deep, aching sorrow mixed with anxiety, mixed with the confusion of not knowing what was going on, and a fear that it wasn't anything good.

I got home and I cooked dinner, but I still hadn't heard from her. I texted her and asked her if she was coming home, and I still didn't get anything back.

I texted her again, asking what was going on and if she was okay. Again, she didn't answer me.

I started reaching out to her friends when it got to nine 9 o'clock that night. When I spoke with Kyra, and she hadn't heard from Emali, she offered to go over to the house in Minot.

She called me after she got there and said, "Heidi, something isn't right."

"What do you mean?"

"Both of the cars are in the driveway." By this time, Emali had purchased a vehicle. Kyra said, "Both of the cars are in the driveway. All of the lights are on in the house. The curtains are drawn, so I can't see anything. But the door is locked and nobody's coming to the door."

"Well, are you just lightly knocking?"

"I'm pounding and I'm shouting and nobody's coming to the door. Do you think that I should call the police?"

That word hit me hard. *Police.*

"What does your gut say?"

"My gut tells me that I need to call the police."

I felt like I had a mouthful of sand. I said, "Okay, hang up the phone and call."

Emali should have answered my calls, she should have answered my Facetime, she should have picked up the phone or answered the door. I decided that she could go ahead and be mad if the cops showed up. If she got angry that we called the cops, she'd simply have to get over it.

So Kyra called and asked for a wellness check, but they said that they were going to be a while because they were really busy. She waited for a long while before she left.

The police got to the house around midnight, according to the police officer that I spoke with that eventually gave me the news. He said that when they went there around midnight, they used full sirens in the driveway and had their flashing lights going. They used their PA system, they pounded on the door, but they weren't able to make contact. But because they were unclear about the owners of the house – I don't know the exact legalities behind it – they didn't force entry.

They called Kyra because Kyra was the one who initially requested the wellness check. They told her all of this, and she called me to tell me what they had said, and that the police officers were going to go back in the morning. They assured her that they were going to call her when they did.

An hour or so after I talked to her, I asked her again if she had heard anything and she said she hadn't.

More than anything, I wanted to go over to that house. But I had the baby and no one else to watch her. On top of all the other concerns, I would have had to wake her up and put her in the car. It made more sense to me to have a friend go over, just in case. Just to check. I thought about how Emali would have been absolutely fuming that I woke her baby up and put her in the car and drove her over there.

At 5.50 the next morning, having heard nothing, I called the sheriff's office and talked to the dispatch. I said, "My daughter's friend called for the welfare check on her around midnight, and you weren't able to make contact, and she told me you're supposed to go back this morning. I haven't heard anything. *She* hasn't heard anything. I need to know what's happening. I haven't heard from her. I haven't heard from you guys. What's going on?"

He put me through to an officer. That officer told me at that point he had just come on duty and read the report from the previous wellness check, and he was alarmed by the fact that there was so much happening and they didn't make contact. Nobody came out of the house at all.

He said, "I'm down the street from the house. I've pulled over so I don't drop our call and I'm waiting for another officer to come meet me here, and then we're going to go and try to make contact again. If we don't make contact, we'll look into forced entry."

It had been hours. By now, I was so distraught that I couldn't even think straight. I was calling him. I called my brother. I called Emali's father. I was hoping that somebody, *anybody* would give me some type of hope, some kind of proof that my gut was wrong - because even though I didn't know, I'm a mom, so I could feel that something wasn't right from the time that I texted her that she had the baby's bubby.

I knew something was wrong, but I couldn't prove it. There's a mother's intuition and then there's going overboard, and if my gut was wrong, I wanted to at least try to stay centered.

I wound up going to work because I had no idea what else I should do. I mean, staying home and staring at the wall didn't seem like an option that would allow me to keep my quickly unraveling sanity. The waiting was horrid, a tension like nothing I'd ever experienced before. I was waiting for a phone call from the police, or a text from my daughter, or a message from one of her friends who would tell me that Emali was fine. I was bouncing back and forth between a faint hope and a crushing despair.

So the only thing that I could think of, the only thing I could do, was my job. I went to work and pretended to go about my day.

Then, they came in. The police. Two sheriffs and two state troopers came into my job, and they told me that Emali was dead. One of them said, "We're so sorry to have to tell you that your daughter is deceased."

It felt like a door slammed shut in my head. I needed to leave, but I wasn't sure where I was going or how to get there - I was sure I couldn't drive anywhere. I left my car at work and got in the cruiser with the officer who I had talked to on the phone earlier in the morning.

He confided that at that time, he wasn't really on the side of the road waiting for an officer. He was at the house in full SWAT gear with a team, just about to force entry when my call came in. He had walked down to the end of the driveway and shut his radio off so I wouldn't hear anything that was happening, then told me that story, and then he went back and forced entry and found them.

SOMEONE RECENTLY ASKED me how someone could absorb the news that their child is dead. All I can say to that is, you don't. I mean, even now, it's still not absorbed. I can't imagine that I'll ever honestly accept it.

Hearing that police officer say that my daughter had been murdered completely broke me. That's not just a phrase: It's truly how I felt, and it's how I feel now.

The only thing that I know how to do is to just keep going. I can't wallow in my own self-pity, because I still have people whom I love and who rely on me. Equally important, though, is that I have to push forward and speak for Emali - because she's not here to speak for herself anymore.

Even now, as I go about my life and I take care of my granddaughter, and I take care of my daughter and my son and my house, and I have my job, someone will tell me something entertaining or I'll see something online - and as crazy as it sounds, I'll forget that she's gone. I'll go to call her on my way home from work or I'll begin to send her a text to check on her, and it hits me again. She's not going to answer me.

Obviously, in my head I know she's not here. But my heart won't let it in, and that moment of remembering that she's gone sears my soul all over again.

I THINK ABOUT WHAT Emali told me about living with her boyfriend, how he got her to stay in his life, and the dark irony of his words makes me sick. She said he would make her feel guilty because he would say that if she left, their child would come from a broken home.

According to Emali, one of his favorite lectures was, "What do you think our kid is going to do later on in life when she has two Christmases and two birthdays, and we're arguing over school vacations? Shouldn't she just have a normal life where both of her parents live together?"

When she finally told me about it, I answered with, "Honey, you can have separate lives and still raise a happy child. You don't have to live miserable. Just having two parents under one roof does *not* automatically create a well-adjusted child. Right now, the only people that are allowed to love that baby are me, you, him, and his mom. How many times can nobody else be around her because he doesn't allow her out of the house? That's not fair to her."

I think that was when she started to really consider her options. In the end, though, he chose to make sure that my granddaughter was an orphan at his hands - which is the ultimate broken home.

Trying to reconcile the irony is an exercise in futility. You can't apply logic to the insanity of all this.

Still, I keep going back to what I think of him. He didn't just flip a switch one day and develop his way of dealing with the world, did he? Were I responsible for him, he would have been medicated. Maybe institutionalized. In my opinion, some type of intervention was needed way earlier. *Something* should have been done before he met my daughter.

That's obvious, of course, seeing as he killed her.

I DON'T HAVE ALL OF the details about Emali's murder. I sometimes think that's a merciful thing, because what I do know is already horrifying, and I don't know what I would do if I had to go the rest of my life with more specifics.

He shot her in the head and then he turned the gun on himself. When we went to see her at the funeral home before the funeral, they had done their best to cover her wound, and it just looked like she had bumped her head.

We did an open casket at first, because we wanted to make sure that everybody could see her, touch her, and kiss her if they wanted to, and say goodbye. It was all so sudden that we didn't want to take that away from the people who loved her.

During the preparation, Eva went in to see her. She came back out and talked to the funeral director and said, "Okay, you have to flat iron her hair and put fake eyelashes on her." She began listing all the things that she wanted the funeral home to do to make Emali look like Emali.

I decided to let Eva stay in that place in her mind. It seemed to be helping her cope. I sent the kids to Portland to buy Emali's burial outfit, and instead of coming back with a sundress or whatever, they came home with gray sweatpants, a gray zip-up hoodie, and a pink crop top.

That was Emali. That's what she would have worn anyway, so that's what we had them put her in. Since she had too many abrasions on her body to have a lot of exposure, in the end it was a good choice. Although the police didn't give me specific details about what had happened to her physically before he took her life, and the funeral home tried to be as compassionate and as discreet as possible, the context of what they did tell me was that he beat her severely before he shot her.

LIFE WILL ALWAYS HAVE this cloud hanging over it. I'm trying to hold everything together for my other children and me, but I also want to make sure that Emali lives on - especially for her daughter's sake. I can't allow her mother to fade away. Emali wasn't that type of person. She was never one to sit in the background, so I won't allow her to be forgotten.

I also want to do whatever I can to make sure that this doesn't happen to others. If I can save a life using Emali's story, then that will enhance the beautiful legacy she was able to create in her short time with us.

If only I'd been there that night. It's possible that wouldn't have changed much of anything, except perhaps my other children would have lost both their sister and their mother, but at least I would have been with her. And I would have stopped him or died trying. When an abused woman is trying to leave, someone needs to be there to protect her. It's the most dangerous time for her.

At some point, I did learn one of the reasons Emali didn't want a police standby on the day she tried to leave: She was afraid of getting into trouble because of their living situation, staying in a trailer that was going through probate court. She thought she would have gotten in trouble for squatting. She didn't want the boyfriend to get in trouble for squatting either, for a couple of different reasons.

One was because she didn't want to be the reason for him to be homeless because then, that would have just given him more fuel to continue to treat her poorly and make her feel guilty. Other than that, she believed that he would have eventually gone to his mother's house, which would have put him closer to my house, and she didn't want that either. She didn't want to bring his drama to me.

She was just trying to take care of it on her own. That's something that a lot of victims do. If there's any type of questionable activity happening in the house, they don't want to get their assailant in trouble - because then, it's *their* fault because they called the police. It just extends the abuse even if they manage to escape, and it's one of the things that needs to change about the ways in which we address DV. We need to make victims feel safe in asking for help.

And that extends to the public, as well. People need to better understand the real dynamics of abuse, and then know what to do once they become aware of it in their midst.

As for the victims, there is one thing they can do that will make a huge difference - and I hope they read this and take it to heart: When the people who love you are telling you that you're in a dangerous relationship, *please trust them*. Listen to what they're saying. They're on the outside, looking in at something that's terrifying them.

But from where they're standing, they can see things that you don't - because the view is clearer from the outside.

"I want to be a weeping willow tree."

Emali had a tattoo on her bicep that was her child's birth flower. After her death, I got a tattoo of two flowers on my bicep: One of them is Emali's birth flower, and the other is her death flower. I put her name in the stem, and then I put the same tattoo that she'd had on her bicep for her baby. I put that on my forearm, but there are voids through it so that it's like the wind. So it's Emali's birth flower and death flower, and then there's wind coming down and wiping away the tattoo that Emali had on her bicep.

I have the year 2005 tattooed on the back of my elbow because this past year, on my birthday, Emali went and got a tattoo of 1985 on the back of her elbow, which is the year that I was born. That was her birthday present to me – her tattoo of my birth year. She sent it to me while I was at work. I don't recall if I told her this, but I cried. It was the sweetest gift I ever got.

There are countless beautiful memories. The impact that Emali had on so many lives... It's immeasurable. But one in particular stays with me every day of my life:

She was scrolling through Facebook a few years ago, and came across a video of a burial option - one where the person's ashes were put into a pod from which they then grew a tree. She thought it was the most amazing thing. She showed it to me and said, "Mommy, this is what I want to do. If anything ever happens to me, like when I'm old and I die, I want to be a weeping willow tree."

No parent ever thinks about what their child wants when they die. But we had to.

Although our state doesn't allow the pod, we do have what they call "green" cemeteries, where we could plant a tree and it's protected - but they're all very far away from where any of Emali's loved ones live.

So we split her ashes. We made a living urn, which is something that our state does offer. We have some of her ashes in one urn, and that's in her plot in the cemetery. She's protected there. And then we have some ashes in a living urn that we are going to bury with a weeping willow tree, in the yard of a house across the street from the cemetery, because that's the house that her father owns.

The plan is that we're going to put her tree in the front yard. Emali's sister Eva is going to be living there soon, like she had planned to do with her sister, and she'll be caring for Emali's tree. So will all the others who so loved Emali.

When Emali's little girl is grown, the house will be hers - with her mother's weeping willow tree in the front yard, watching over her.

In loving memory of Emali Renee Sallee
March 10, 2005-April 10, 2024